The Borderline Mom

A Quick & Dirty Manual of Emotional Self
Defense for Children

By Georgiana Wright

Contents

Introduction

I got home around 10PM from my date. Understand, I was twenty-two at the time, I didn't have a curfew or anything. When I came in she was sitting at the kitchen table in the dark, waiting. I was about to say how sweet it was for her to still wait up for me, when she sprang to her feet and slapped me across the mouth.

I just froze. She hadn't had a bad episode in a while but I was familiar with them. I didn't want to open my mouth until I heard whatever crazy thing she had to say about why she slapped me. I racked my brain trying to think of anything I could have possibly done to upset her. She hissed, "What do you have to say for yourself, you slut?"

I always said I'd keep my wits about me the next time, I wouldn't give her anything to use against me but I always failed. "Wha-what?" I stammered. I'd been dating the same guy for two years, and we'd just gone out to dinner... Mom and I had had a nice chat about him before I left three hours ago, actually.

"DON'T PLAY DUMB YOU LITTLE WHORE. DO YOU THINK I DON'T KNOW WHAT YOU'VE BEEN DOING?!"

I burst into tears. Less because of the accusation than the fact that She was back. Evil Mom, I called her in my head, when I was a little girl. The one who would slap me silly for whispering in church, when I hadn't made a sound. The one who would accuse me of turning Dad "against" her, or of hiding drugs. I prayed I could think of the right thing to say, to do, to calm her down. I prayed I wouldn't do anything to make this worse.

It would have been easier, almost, if she'd been Evil Mom full-time. Less confusing. But when Evil Mom wasn't around, she was so good to me, said things that made me believe she loved me. Made me love her so much it hurt to think about.

Collateral Damage

People with borderline personality disorder (BPD) suffer. But the people around them suffer as much, if not more, when their behaviors reach terroristic levels of emotional and psychological mayhem. When faced with someone like this, instinctive responses fail you.

The fear and pain someone with BPD can inflict on their loved ones, even if it's not a conscious choice, can be emotionally and psychologically devastating. Some borderline personalities resort to physical violence. Others depend on psychological means of controlling and manipulating their loved ones. While BPD can present in many different ways, the survivors of relationships with borderline personality disordered individuals have much in common. Regardless of the specific means your borderline personality disordered mother used to manipulate and control your life, her sickness bred confusion and instability during your formative years.

Borderline personalities view emotional bonds, family attachments, and other commitments, as leverage. Wracked by irrational fears, they will attempt to use this leverage to control their environment, including their family members and friends. To the borderline personality, this behavior is justified—she constantly feels threatened, abandoned, or under attack, and is unable to accept that it is in fact her own "justified behavior" causing the chaos that surrounds her.

No one has more emotional and psychological leverage over us than our own mothers. The combination of borderline personality disorder and parental responsibility is a particularly tragic one. There are few people in our lives that hold a role as pivotal as our mothers do, for as long as we live. And for a mother, her child is, or should be, just as important.

This presents a problem when the mother is a borderline personality. There are two general ways (with infinite variations) that borderline personality disorder may disrupt the maternal/child relationship. Although these ways are seemingly completely opposite, they stem from the same cause.

Some borderline personality mothers are excessively involved with their children. This involvement itself takes many forms. She may have an obsession with her child's success, for example. Or she may harbor an equally powerful obsession with her child's perceived disobedience. Her life may revolve around praising the child, or around castigating the child unfairly. In either case, the child holds a central role in her life, and she exhibits an unhealthy dependence upon her ability to control the child.

Yet a mother with the same disorder may also neglect her child. Her child may seem invisible to her. She is absent as a mother, a teacher, a friend, a support of any kind. This type of borderline personality disordered woman is not interested in controlling or disciplining her child at all. She does not praise As on the report card, or notice Fs. She may notice if the child does something which cannot fail to interrupt her own lifestyle, but otherwise, she may as well be childless.

These opposite styles are not mutually exclusive, either. Some mothers with BPD see-saw between them; a mother may be obsessive about her infant and then seem to 'forget' that obsession when her child reaches school age—or she may change from week to week, day to day, hour to hour.

In this book, we will discuss what BPD really is. We'll cover the traits which borderline personalities exhibit, and discuss the effects of being exposed to these traits at a formative age. Understanding the root of these behaviors through understanding borderline personality disorder itself cannot erase the pain you've experienced. Nor can we outline a cure for your mother. But this understanding can serve another purpose. Healing.

We learn about the world, what to expect from it, and how it works, from our parents. Learning from a borderline personality mother, whose own world view is distorted, paranoid, or delusional cannot help but be traumatic. Part of readjusting your own world view is to understand what is or was wrong with *hers.*

That understanding can help you recognize the behaviors which have caused you so much pain. Understanding helps you see the world from a perspective outside that you grew up with, and helps you recognize manipulation, isolation, and abuse for what they are: things which you cannot and must not tolerate.

Why Understanding of BPD is Critical

> *I'll never forget it. I was eight years old and it was Mother's Day. I got out of bed and crept downstairs and made a bowl of cereal, buttered toast with jelly, poured a glass of milk, made coffee... carried it all upstairs on a tray for her. I set the tray down by the door and jumped into bed with her. I was so glad it was Mother's Day and I could do something to cheer her up!*
>
> *"Mommy! Wake up! I have a surprise for you!" I squealed. I reached over and turned on the light. "It's breakfast in bed!" I hopped down and picked up the tray.*

She smiled at me, and gave me a hug. I curled up beside her and she petted my hair.

"If I didn't have you, angel," she said, "I think Mommy would kill herself. Don't ever leave me, okay? Never."

"Of course I won't leave you, Mommy," I replied. The scariest thing about this memory isn't that she said she'd kill herself without me, but that I didn't think it was a strange thing for her to say. Mom had told me before about how people could kill themselves with pills or razors or guns if they were sad. I decided I'd never, ever let her be sad.

Borderline personality disorder is a complex mental illness that is only recently becoming more understood, in terms of its causes and internal mechanisms, and much about the disease remains a mystery.

The traits and behaviors exhibited by those with BPD, however, are easily identifiable. They lead to a chronic, repetitive cycle of disruption in relationships, unstable identity, and unpredictable moods. Through these traits and tendencies, borderline personalities are prone to impulsive and often dangerous or damaging behavior, and emotional or even physical acts of violence.

These traits can be damaging to almost any relationship or contact one has with someone who has the disorder. The closer the relationship, and the more central that relationship is to the life of either party, the more havoc the disorder can wreak upon both individuals.

These traits can lead those who love borderline personality disordered persons to experience intense levels of anxiety, guilt, fear, sadness and anger. But it is not only BPDs ability to affect the emotions of those whose lives are touched by it that makes it such a dangerous disorder.

The behaviors of the borderline personality disordered can have equally destructive effects on others lives in much more concrete ways. Borderline personality disorder does indeed have the capacity to ruin lives, both of those who have the disorder, and those who come into contact with them. The children, parents, and spouses of BPs face enormous challenges in coping with the effects the disorder has on their loved ones and on their own lives.

The basic traits we are about to discuss are the foundation for the behaviors you have witnessed as the child of a borderline personality disordered mother.

These traits are not outlined as an excuse for the abuse, control, isolation, neglect, or manipulations you were subject to; that is not the purpose for exploring them here.

Instead our purpose is to build your understanding. Our purpose is to give you some answers for *why,* why these behaviors took place, because she cannot or will not give you those answers herself. Our purpose is to give you a new perspective, outside of the perspective your mother may have tried to enforce, that perspective which revolved around her. And finally, but most importantly, our purpose is to give you the necessary tools to live a safer, healthier life.

Sarah's Story

It wasn't until I was much older, in my thirties, that I realized that there was something terribly wrong with the way my mother saw me. My entire life, up to then, I thought it was me. I knew it, actually.

You might wonder, if you knew my mother, how anyone could miss it. Even a child. She wasn't very good at playing normal.

But I knew it was me, because... I was the one she hated. I mean, I had an older sister and a younger brother—but she didn't hate them. My sister was her golden child. Everything she did was perfect. My little brothers were... kind of off her radar, I guess.

But not me. I was the one she hit. I was the one who got locked up. I was the one who wasn't allowed to eat at the table, or ask for help with homework. I was the one who she called names, who she accused of awful things.

I could never see past how much she hated me, I guess, to see everything else that was wrong.

After all this time, I still don't understand. I understand that she was sick. Is still sick. But why was I singled out?

-Sarak K.

Sarah's situation is a difficult one to come to terms with, and one that is unfortunately all too common in households controlled by a mother with borderline personality disorder.

The behaviors a borderline personality exhibits are symptoms. You can think of her behaviors, her actions, as the path she chose in order to cope with *her* sickness.

Sarah's mother didn't have a problem with *Sarah,* and it wasn't that she "didn't" have a problem with Sarah's siblings.

Understanding borderline personality disorder when we're not part of the situation is difficult enough; understanding it when we *are* part of the situation can be even harder. The important thing to understand is that the BP mother's "problem" was, and is, with *herself.*

For those with borderline personality disorder who seek recovery, understanding this is paramount. Many BPs project their difficulties onto the people around them. If the borderline personality feels fear of abandonment, she may accuse her loved ones of abandoning her. If she fears being controlled, she may accuse them of controlling her—regardless of whether or not that fear is based on reality.

At this point in her life, Sarah's probably starting to understand that, but she still wonders why she was singled out among the others.

Unfortunately, that's a question to which she may never know the full answer. The borderline personality disorder tendency toward black and white thinking means that almost anything could have triggered the initial idea that Sarah was the 'bad' child.

It almost certainly had nothing to do with Sarah herself. It could have been that her mother didn't feel ready to have another child yet, or that she was a colicky baby, or that she had a bad day the day she found out she was pregnant. It could have been that Sarah reminded her of herself—or that she didn't.

Ultimately, though, the precise trigger doesn't really matter, because the cause of her behavior was BPD and her inability to cope constructively. It may seem unfair, say it doesn't matter—it had a huge effect on Sarah's life, after all.

Yet, if Sarah can come to terms with this, the idea that her mother's arbitrary judgment was a function of the disorder and not of Sarah herself, this understanding may be the factor that truly liberates her from her past.

Chapter 1
The Traits of Borderline Personality Disorder

Black and White Thinking, Self-defined Reality

One of the most significant traits of borderline personality disorder is the tendency toward black and white thinking. For many borderline personalites, there are no shades of grey. Whether the target is a person or a situation, the BP may classify the target as "all good" or "all bad" to an unrealistic or even delusional extent.

The desire to cling to this oversimplified point of view may lead a BP to ignore or reject reality. The emotional and psychological upheavals that these classifications must necessarily cause create chaos. Because the borderline personality worldview is so inflexible, any attempt by an outsider to temper these emotional reactions with reason is resisted.

Not only is the perspective of the borderline personality inflexible and often irrational, it is self-centered. This is a natural consequence of the fact that the BP *defines* her own reality. For most of us, our emotions are a response to the situations we find ourselves in, though they are naturally influenced by our pasts and our beliefs as well. But a borderline personality's emotional response does not always match up to the reality with which she is confronted. Rather than evaluate her own emotional response in an appropriate reality, she's likely to simply reject the reality at hand, adopting instead a version of reality which justifies her own emotions. .

Identity and Personality Crises

Another trademark of borderline personality disorder is ongoing identity crisis. Those diagnosed with borderline personality disorder may describe themselves as "empty," "needing to fill a void," and so forth. Filling this perceived void or distracting from perceived emptiness becomes a driving force in the BP's life.

There are a number of characteristic methods a BP may use to address this feeling. These methods may include personality "makeovers," for example. A new hobby becomes a new obsession, as the borderline personality tries to extract a sense of self from the activity. Religious conversions, sudden political or philosophical fervor, or other ideological shifts sometimes play a role in their "makeover." This type of BP may also seek to form an identity based on her career, her role as a mother or wife, or anything else she views as offering a ready-made personality that she may step into.

Some borderline personalities may cycle through these personas quickly. She may present herself as an artist one week, and a career woman the next, necessitating a whole new wardrobe and outlook on life. She may obsessively make all of her child's meals from scratch for several months, but when the domestic-caregiver "personality" fails to soothe her anxiety over the emptiness inside, she abandons it abruptly, and it's back to TV dinners. For others, these adopted personas may last months or years, though that is not necessarily healthier, as she is still substituting the manufactured persona should be for a true sense of self.

Reckless and Dangerous Behavior

Self destructive behavior is common among those with borderline personality disorder. Not only are these behaviors *self* destructive, they can have a significant impact on the lives of those associated with the borderline personality, also.

These behaviors often stem from the BP's identity crisis, or are a response to her battle against reality. Some of these behaviors seem impulsive, others seem compulsive. Some borderline personalities have unsafe sexual habits, others engage in substance abuse. Some may hide gambling addictions, or compulsively overspend.

These behaviors, and many others, may be intended to vent the BP's frustration, garner attention, or serve as way to punish herself or others. They may also feed the BP's hunger for drama, intended to ease the emptiness within.

All of these behaviors may signify or at least symbolize a loss of control. But certain types of reckless behavior may create complications that become just as disruptive as, or even more disruptive than borderline personality disorder itself.

Suicidal and Self-Harm Tendencies

In desperation and frustration, borderline personalities turn to suicide threats or attempts, or self-injuring behaviors.

Suicide threats may serve as a tool to manipulate those around them, or to express the severity of their distress. The same can be said of self-harming behaviors, like head banging, or cutting or burning themselves. Like other dangerous and harmful behaviors the borderline personality adopts, these are not only a way for the BP to punish herself, but a way to punish others or to guarantee their care and attention.

Threatening suicide can seem—to a borderline personality—to be an excellent method for getting her way. By threatening suicide, she is basically holding herself hostage until her demands are fulfilled; by doing so, she lays out an ultimatum. If the target for this ultimatum doesn't respond the way the BP wishes, she can accuse him or her of not loving her, not caring if she is alive or dead. In this way, suicide threats and self harm may become a form of emotional blackmail the BP uses against her family and friends. Some borderline personalities will even use this as a way to control their children. A borderline mother who uses suicide threats to control her child is forcing a role reversal, demanding that the child take responsibility for *her* well-being rather than vice versa.

Fear of Abandonment

Fear of abandonment looms large for BPs, and they will go to drastic lengths to avoid abandonment, whether it is real or imagined.

Part of this fear stems from the weak sense of self the BP feels. Her insecurity contributes to her sense of instability. The fact that she cannot control other people, and cannot force them to accept her version of reality is intolerable. Anyone with a strong sense of self is perceived as a type of threat, even if she loves them. Simply because she knows she can't "make" someone love her, "make" them stay, she is compelled to try.

None of us can make others love us, of course. Nor can we force others to remain a part of our lives. For most of us, this is simply the way the world works, and we wouldn't want to change it. After all, it is what makes close relationships so special, so precious. We *choose* to contribute to one another's lives; we *choose* to share our time, our affection, and our energy with one another.

Unfortunately, this is a reality that many BPs either cannot or will not accept. The weak sense of self that haunts the BP creates an inherent insecurity and instability; contributing to this is the discord between her own emotional life and reality.

To compensate for her insecurity, the BP attempts to exert control. Other people, of course, cannot be directly or completely controlled. What cannot be controlled, tailored to her perception of reality, the borderline personality cannot trust. This distrust feeds into and magnifies her fears of abandonment.

Paranoid Ideation, Delusional Beliefs, Magical Thinking

All of these traits—the lack of self control, the weak sense of self, the intensity of emotion, and the attempt to make reality match her volatile inner world result can in paranoid ideation, sometimes to the point of delusional beliefs.

This paranoia can have severe consequences on the lives of those around her. BPs may accuse their children and other loved ones of such fantastical schemes that there is no realistic defense; they may believe in their accusations despite being presented with definitive evidence to the contrary. Borderline personalities will also attempt to enlist their family members, when consumed with paranoid regarding others. They create division within the family and use this division to manipulate or isolate certain important people in their lives.

Magical thinking is another trait that the borderline personality disordered may present. Magical thinking is the concept that thoughts and emotions may directly affect reality. An example of magical thinking would be believing that someone you got into an argument with had a traffic accident because you were angry with that person. This may seem far-fetched, or childish, but keep in mind that the BP is often (though perhaps not consciously) trying to tailor the outside world to fit her inside world. Considered in this light, magical thinking— from a borderline personality perspective, at least— makes tragic sense.

Chapter 2
Growing up with a Borderline Personality Mother

For adults, coping with a friend, relative, or partner who has borderline personality disorder is a challenge. It can be frustrating. It leads to anger, heartbreak, confusion, guilt, and anxiety.

This is true, too, of adults whose mothers are borderline personality disordered, of course. But there is also the additional complication, in that scenario, of having been *raised* by a BP.

Our emotional fortitude, our ability to distinguish what is real, our concepts of responsibility and love, of affection, of trust, are all strongly influenced by our parents. We cannot help but to trust what they say, in the beginning, because we have no other option. And their opinions of us carry weight, even if we have outgrown the need to agree with them.

For adult children of borderline personality disordered mothers, remembering childhood is painful and confusing. When one's reality revolves around Mom, but Mom's reality revolves only around herself and her own emotions, the results are chaotic and often traumatic.

The traits and symptoms characteristic of borderline personality disorder do not excuse the suffering you have experienced. Calling it a disorder does not absolve her. But understanding how and why some events came about *can* help to ease some of your own pain, your own guilt, your own anxiety.

When their parents are in pain, children often blame themselves, even if their parents wish they wouldn't. Unfortunately, a borderline personality mother may actually reinforce a child's fear that he or she is responsible for the mother's well-being or happiness, that the child is to blame for the mother's difficulties.

Reassessing Your Childhood

As has already been discussed, borderline personality disorder severely affects the ability to parent. The ways in which borderline personality disorder affects the mother child/relationship are numerous, and vary from family to family. But the root cause of the dissonance is always the same.

Borderline personalities seem to exist in a state of contradiction. Despite her underdeveloped sense of self, the borderline personality mother is extremely self-absorbed. Though this may seem contradictory, the lack of a strong sense of self is what fuels her obsessions and her behaviors. Unable to feel content or secure with herself in reality, she strives to create a reality which will furnish her with the stability she craves.

But she doesn't go about this in a rational or practical way, because her emotions are irrational and out of control. Rather than re-evaluate her own state of mind, she struggles to justify her lack of control and her inner emptiness by blaming, denying, or attempting to manipulate the reality that surrounds her into a fantasy that justifies her inner chaos.

Unfortunately, her child is a significant player in that reality—and one over which she has a great deal of practical control.

This control may be exercised as either an excess of attention, or as neglect. She may be consistent in her obsession—or her neglect—or these forms of abuse may alternate, a cycle of anxiety and uncertainty for her child.

Being the center of her obsession can be terrifying. Her black and white thinking brands a child as all-good, or as a all-bad. Yet, even being her angel is a frightening level of responsibility for a child. Failing her impossibly high expectations, the expectations on which her happiness and well-being seem to depend, is unthinkable.

The child she sees as being a "bad" child, however, she treats as irredeemable. No matter what this child does, no matter what he or she accomplishes, the mother's opinion is set in stone.

If the child is not the focus of her obsessions, then the child may instead seem to be virtually invisible to her. This may sound preferable to the child endlessly vilified, but in fact this emotional abandonment is equally abusive in its own way. And just as her obsessive attention can sometimes lead to physical abuse, her disinterest may pave the way to physical neglect.

There is little middle ground with a BP; that goes not only for what is all-good versus what is all-bad. It applies both to what she finds important and what she completely ignores.

In any case, her attention or her disinterest is dictated by her own self-involvement: her drive to fill the internal void that haunts her. If the child is a threat to her *preferred* version of reality, the child is considered a monster, without regard for any other factors. For the mother who perceives the child as an answer to her emptiness, or a surrogate through which she can achieve recognition and identity, the child can do no wrong.

And many children subjected to a mother with experience a roller coaster of positive and negative obsessive attention which could change to neglect and disinterest with whiplash speed.

Borderline mothers may present themselves in wildly variable fashion—variation from day to day, and also from individual to individual—but they all have one thing in common. The love given by a borderline personality is never unconditional.

Her love always comes with conditions, and her conditions are always based on the demands of her inner fantasy, the reality she chooses to believe in because it justifies her emotional chaos and otherwise unjustifiable actions.

Giving birth does not make a woman into a mother. Being called "Mom" doesn't make her a mother. Mothers love unconditionally; not only did your mother have conditions for her love, but when they weren't met you faced verbal abuse, hatred, rage, soul-numbing neglect, wild tears, blame...

Not only did she impose conditions, but they were wildly arbitrary, ever changing, and sometimes impossible to comprehend or even detect.

What this Understanding Means for You as an Adult

You've been trapped in a cycle of love and hate, forced to try and meet her emotional needs, as she tries to warp reality any way she possibly can to match her inner turmoil. Our mothers should be our source of comfort and support, should teach us about affection and appropriate behavior. But a borderline mother cannot and does not do these things.

Mothers are supposed to want, more than anything, the best for their children. They want their children to be safe, secure, happy, and confident. They're supposed to *teach* us how to be these things. But a borderline mother teaches only fear, guilt, and obligation.

She's tried her best to control you, instead of teaching you confidence. She's threatened your mental and physical well-being, instead of making you safe and teaching you safety. She's made your happiness dependant on hers—which is unpredictable or even non-existent. In fact, she often resists happiness, when the opportunity to embrace it is presented.

The children of BPs, as they grow older themselves, as they become adults, often begin to understand that their mothers were ill. This breeds a new type of ambivalence. If she is ill, perhaps it wasn't her fault? Perhaps anger or frustration is not acceptable? How should one cope with her irrational, controlling, or cruel tendencies now?

Adult children of borderline personality disordered mothers know that appeasing her doesn't work. Yet, they often fear the consequences of resisting her manipulation. This fear is not necessarily self-preservation. Sometimes it is, but just as often, they fear *for* her. They fear that she may harm herself. They are afraid of hurting her.

For some of you, coming to the understanding that your mother is disordered—is *ill*—has helped you come to terms with your childhood. But in the process, it has left you feeling more ambivalent about how to deal with your mother in the *present*.

It feels wrong to be angry or resentful of someone who is ill. One questions over and over "Can she *help it?* Is it even *possible* for her to understand the world in a different way, to behave more appropriately?"

These are meaningful questions, but they are questions your mother must find the answers to, herself. Through treatment, counseling, and self-motivation, BPs have successfully sought recovery. Her recovery, however, *is* not and *cannot* be your responsibility. This isn't only for your own good—it is for hers as well. Understanding and motivating herself, imposing self-discipline: these are key elements in the process of recovering from BPD. Other than steering her toward professional help, you cannot help her to recover.

But there are other things you can and must do, for yourself, and these things can—if she allows them to—be a first step in that direction for her.

You must not allow her disorder to rule or ruin your life anymore. You must not submit to her sickness, or appease it.

This book is about learning to defend yourself, against her sickness, her actions, her manipulations. This book is about taking responsibility for your own well being.

It isn't, of course, fair that you have to defend yourself at all. And in some cases, putting an end to the relationship is the only option. That, of course, is for you to decide.

We'll first discuss some ways to identify typical borderline personality disorder behaviors that she uses, and the appropriate ways to react to these behaviors. We'll explore the critical importance of boundaries, and ways for you to counteract and defend yourself against typical borderline tactics. Our methods are intended to both protect you and to improve your relationship with her, if she'll cooperate. If she refuses to cooperate, these same methods should help to defuse situations.

Isolation, abuse, manipulation—these are things which you should not fall prey to. Succumbing to her in these ways does not help her. We hope that this text will give you both light and direction in the often dark and confusing labyrinth BPs are capable of constructing.

But the most important thing this book is about is *you.* Your safety. Your emotional, psychological, and physical well-being. The difficulty of being involved in the life of someone with BPD does not come only from her behaviors toward you, but in the long term effects those behaviors and attitudes have had on you.

Having a borderline personality mother can make you believe that your own life can't improve unless she is better; thankfully that is not true. Hers *may* improve once you begin to work on being happy and healthy yourself, but in the end, it is her choice whether or not that is the case.

What is absolutely certain, however, is that the situation will *not* improve—for either of you—as long as you are at the mercy of her moods and borderline personality influenced traits. Allowing her to rule the relationship results in a never-ending cycle of appeasement, growing dissatisfaction, upping the ante, and continuing disregard for boundaries.

Chapter 3
Should I Stay, or Should I Go?

Learning to make your own safety, security, and well-being a priority is not a simple thing to do when you were raised by a borderline personality disordered mother. During your childhood, you absorbed the lesson that your needs, your well being, and your safety were secondary to hers. You were constantly shown, implicitly and explicitly that *you* were secondary to her.

Even for those who were favored, golden children of BP mothers, this message was paramount. Even if their successes and accomplishments were obsessed over and doted upon and bragged about, they were inculcated with the understanding that these accomplishments reflected upon their mother. That she *depended* upon them.

We must each learn to make our individual wellness a priority. This doesn't mean not making sacrifices for others, or not being a giving person. It means that to have any hope of being a support or a comfort to another person, we must first be well ourselves.

> *Long ago I started making decisions about what to do based on how I thought Mom would react. I told myself it wasn't about being afraid of her, but just being responsive to her needs. Or "not causing trouble." Or "not rocking the boat."*

The thing is, it just kept snowballing. Each sacrifice seemed small at the time—worthwhile if it meant avoiding a tantrum from her, or not inciting her unpredictable rage, or not making her cry. "It's not a big deal," became my mantra when it came to giving things up.

"Oh, I can't go out this weekend, Mom would be lonely. It's not a big deal."

"No, I should get off the phone now—Mom will be home and you know how she gets when I talk to you, Dad. It's not a big deal, I'll call you tomorrow when she's at work."

"Yeah, Mom said some things she said that she shouldn't have... it hurt my feelings... but it's okay, I didn't take it to heart, really. She seems to be over it now, anyway. Better to just let it slide."

That was bad enough but then at some point she became so used to having me tiptoe around her moods that if I expressed even uncertainty about doing exactly what she wanted, even in the smallest things, she would fly into a rage.

You Can't be a Lifeguard When You're Drowning

This is important to understand not because the "point" of you helping yourself is to help your borderline mother, but because you have learned, your entire life, to address her needs and expectations before your own. Even if it's something you no longer want or even consciously try to avoid doing, it has become habitual to forego your own desires and needs in deference to hers.

It may be more of a reflex than a conscious decision, or you may actually consider how anything you do will make her react before you do it. It may be motivated by the fact that you want to help her or it may be motivated by the fact that you want to avoid creating a situation she'll negatively respond to. But the result is the same.

In short, you've been trained.

Caring for yourself is not about being selfish. It's about having a secure, strong, healthy position from which you can see situations clearly and make appropriate decisions and take action in a positive manner.

Your mother didn't teach you to think in this way. Part of the reason for that is, of course, her preoccupation with her fragmenting inner world. The chaotic void she possesses in lieu of a strong sense of self.

But also, in a very real sense, she *couldn't* teach you to think this way—not because of her preoccupation but because true self-preservation, healthy self-care is inconceivable to her. Without a true sense of self, she can't care for her *self* in that way.

> *I know how she treats me isn't right. And I know her reactions are way out of line. But I also know that she's sick, she can't help it. She's the one who needs to be taken care of, she's the one with the illness. If I don't take care of her, if I don't help her, who will?*

> *It means putting up with a lot, that's true, but she's incapable of behaving appropriately. It's just the way she is; I'm the one who needs to learn to deal with it, and learn not to set her off. If I were more careful about that, we'd have fewer fights.*

> *I do get depressed... and it does hurt. But she doesn't mean for it to be that way. I know I have some issues to work on but I just can't stand to see her suffer.*

How—and whether or not –the relationship can continue depends strongly upon this. That is, whether or not it is possible to be involved in your mother's life without endangering your own health.

Making yourself a priority and making healthy decisions about your relationship with your mother can't happen unless you are prepared for the *possibility* that you may have to walk away from the situation.

You have to accept responsibility for yourself and your well-being, and in doing so, you *must* accept that you cannot be responsible for her actions. No relationship can survive if both parties do not contribute; no relationship, not even a maternal-child relationship, can rest on the shoulders of one party.

Even if you are "perfect," even if you sacrifice everything, do everything "right," your mother may simply refuse to be a participant in a relationship that does not allow her to control you.

And if that is the case, breaking off communication is the only option you have, the only option that allows you to be whole and healthy. And the only option which does not enable her, or exacerbate her issues. It may even be the option that saves the relationship—but you have to save yourself *first.*

It Takes Two

There are, of course, two people upon whom the future of this relationship rests: you and your mother.

You

On your part, it depends on changing your perspective and priorities. You must learn to see your safety and quality of life as paramount, which involves facing down the belief instilled in you since childhood that your happiness depends upon hers. This has to be done by implementing *and enforcing* boundaries which protect you from being influenced by her manipulation.

Her

On her part, it depends upon the willingness to learn and cooperate with healthy boundaries, and the willingness to accept that healthy boundaries are not negotiable. That healthy boundaries are not dependent upon her mood, that adherence to them is not conditional upon her level of distress, and that these boundaries are permanent.

At first glance, you may think, "Then there's no hope." After all, her behaviors have long been characterized by an apparently complete and total disregard for at least the emotional (if not also the physical) boundaries of other people. She has demonstrated again and again that she feels that riding roughshod over the psychological and emotional well-being of her children and others in her life is justifiable. Or she completely denies that she ignores boundaries at all. She's demonstrated over and over that she believes her actions at any given time are beyond reproach. If she does admit wrongdoing later, then her guilt is given center stage and she expects you to soothe her, compensate for her guilt, even to take it on yourself.

This may or may not remain the case when boundaries are set and enforced firmly. But you may be surprised at how much can be accomplished with consistent firmness on your part. Reasoning with your BP mother has almost certainly already proven to be infuriating and fruitless, due to her inability to empathize with anyone else's feelings when she herself is out of control.

However, with a slightly different approach, you may experience different results. Your own reinforced sense of self can serve as an example to her, rather than as an obstacle. Many BPs actually crave structure and stability; this type of borderline personality may recognize that she is out of control, and responds well to consistent boundaries that help her to maintain control over her behavior.

Even if she does attempt to cooperate, however, standing up to her is not a simple and easy fix for a relationship which has been plagued with a lifetime of problems. This relationship has been wounded by the chaos and drama of borderline personality disorder; there is no cut and dried procedure that will change that.

Instead of a "solution," this method offers a process. This process has no definite end in sight because the end depends on the personal choices of two people. You can seek, and succeed in the search for, your own personal improvement, but there is no way to guarantee the effect that this process will have on your *relationship.*

The commitment it requires on your part and the responsibility you must assume to carry it out is no small burden. While every relationship in our lives requires maintenance, we generally should not have to constantly remind those we love that their feelings are not a justifiable reason to cause us terrible harm. Yet this process does in fact ask you to fulfill this responsibility in one way. You take responsibility for telling her *no,* and that is a responsibility you should not have to face.

But as you enter this process, you are also putting down a terrible burden. You are laying down the impossible responsibility she laid on you as a child: the burden of being responsible for *her.* For her life, her self, her happiness, and her sanity.

In a Perfect World

In a perfect world, we would not have to say *no* so much, because those we cared for would not demand of us those things for which that answer is required. And even in a less than perfect world, we would expect our parents, our mothers, to understand that concept.

To expect that of a mother with borderline personality disorder, however, is futile. You must accept that her evaluation of how things "should be" may never parallel how what is truly ideal; that even her perception of how things *are* is often tragically out of sync. In accepting this, you also accept that you will have to resist her attempt to force you to see things from her perspective. Or at least, the attempt to force you into *acting* like you do.

The fairytale ending would have her recognizing all of this, realizing it at the deepest level, and changing herself. In the fairytale ending, her understanding would be complete and instant; she would never regress. And in turn, she would make amends for the years of pain already passed; she would comfort you, and heal you, she would untangle the confusion, and erase all of the pain.

The past can't be changed. But the present can be improved and the future can be transformed.

Some people recover from borderline personality disorder. Whether or not your mother will, however, is something you cannot control. Her recovery can never be your main focus, here. Before you could hope to

37

contribute to her recovery—something that only she can choose—you yourself must recover *from her.*

The hard truth is that being involved in the life of a borderline personality, and having that person involved in *your* life is dangerous. You can't put off caring for yourself until she admits she's in the wrong. No amount of martyring yourself is going to make her see the light. If your pain and your suffering could make her change, it would have happened by now.

> *It got to the point where the resentment I felt towards her was just incredible. I knew by then that I was enabling her, that I wasn't really trying to fix things, but I felt helpless... and angry. Sure, it was awful, her screaming at me every day. But SHE is the mother. I felt that eventually she'd HAVE to realize what she was doing. I mean, she HAD to understand how much she was hurting me, right?*

> *I had this fantasy that one day she'd notice that I was crying and not call me drama queen or say I was trying to make her look bad, that the light would come on upstairs and she'd run over to give me a hug and apologize.*

> *And every time that didn't happen, the resentment would grow a little bit stronger, a little bit deeper. At this point I don't know how I'd react even if my fantasy DID come true. I'm not even sure I want it too anymore. I'm not sure I could forgive her for not realizing sooner.*

Making yourself subordinate to a BP is not going to improve the situation. To you, it may seem that you're making sacrifices for her happiness, and the logical conclusion is that she will recognize and appreciate that and change as a result.

That's not going to happen. Accepting her inappropriate behaviors will not improve things for the same reasons that using logic to try and influence her choices doesn't work. Borderline personality disorder is a severe mental illness. No matter how heroic your self-sacrifice is, no matter how profound your persuasive talents, you can't change her point of view as long as the behavior that hurts you continues unchecked. Even *if* either of those things had any potential to succeed over the long-term—which they do not—the present situation is too dangerous and damaging to allow it to continue as is.

If you're reading this book, you've probably already made the decision to try and maintain a relationship with her. It is a risky decision but it is understandable. She is, after all, your mother. Being in her life and having her in yours may eventually make both of your lives better, richer, more fulfilling. However, no matter how easy it *should* be, it *won't* be easy.

Opening Your Eyes to the Present Situation

The first thing you need to do is take a long, hard look at the state of things right now. Assess the injury she's already dealt you, emotionally and psychologically. Assess your ability to set good boundaries and enforce them. Assess the history of the relationship and think about her likely responses to your prioritizing your well-being. You can't predict the future but you probably can determine whether or not you are in immediate danger. You can't tell for certain how she'll respond to boundaries, but you can try to honestly evaluate whether or not you're capable of setting them and enforcing them.

Seeking professional help with this process is also advisable, especially at this beginning stage when your own perceptions are still skewed by her influence. It may help you build confidence in your own intuitions, and it gives you a third party perspective on the circumstances you're dealing with. It would probably be helpful if she would participate in this discussion through family therapy, but seeing a therapist, counselor, or psychologist on your own is also worthwhile.

Your Decisions Don't Need to be Extreme or Irreversible

The second thing you need to do, assuming you continue contact, is determine how limited or involved that contact should be. It isn't unusual for the child of a borderline parent to begin to subscribe to black and white thinking him- or herself; after all, we learn to approach situations by first emulating our parents, and then by compensating for them.

Your mother may well present the options as being a choice only between "none whatsoever" and "whatever she dictates." In fact, these may well be the only options she can imagine. That is not, however, the true reality of the situation. The amount and type of contact in the relationship can be adjusted in numerous ways. You can take the lead here, both in being an example of more realistic thinking, and in differentiating your thought processes from her reality. It is important not only for her to see that there are other options, but for *you* to recognize that you have the capacity to understand certain situations in your own way. You are not enslaved to *her* reality.

And if the relationship you have with your mother is going to continue and improve, diverging from the black-and-white dichotomy she tends to demand is the first step. The eventual development of a fruitful and caring relationship is far more possible if you can employ caution while challenging the relationship. This may mean that involvement needs to be strictly limited, not completely eliminated. An all or nothing attitude may only perpetuate the influence that her disorder has already had on your relationship with one another.

Limited contact can allow for the possibility of more contact once boundaries have been honored consistently. Even taking a break from contact altogether can facilitate a future renewal of contact. The important thing to understand is that you must be willing to concentrate on *current* situation. For the children of BPD parents, sacrificing the present to prevent catastrophe in the future becomes habitual. That habit, however, must change.

Gambling on the future is not the same as hope. Hope is the knowledge that things always *can* improve. Hopes for the future are best defended and made possible by our responsible and thoughtful actions in the present. When we approach our current situation carefully and with resolution, with actions appropriate to the *present*, then hope can open doors for a better future.

If the current situation dictates limited contact, then limiting contact becomes the best way of making more open contact possible. If, however, we don't act with care in the present according to what is necessary and appropriate, a future that includes a better relationship becomes all the more remote and unlikely.

Lauren's Story

I'm not proud of how I walked away. But I am proud that I stayed away.

Someone asked me, "Where'd you find the strength to leave?"

Actually? It wasn't strength at all. It was plain, simple fear. But every other time I'd run away from her, the fear had also driven me back.

So what made this time different? I don't know, exactly. I think part of it was just the ridiculousness I felt when I showed up at my friend Shanna's apartment. It was 3 AM. She'd gotten home not long before, with her boyfriend; it was a Friday night.

She answered the door right away, not realizing at first that I was a wreck.

"Hey girl, did you finally decide to get out and have some fun for once? Want a drink or some coffee? I'm about to put a pot on."

She'd started walking toward the kitchenette already, but my lack of response made her look back.

Here I was, 32 years old, standing in my best friend's doorway... in my pajamas. At least I'd had a coat in my car. Unfortunately, I hadn't had shoes.

"Okay... get in here, tell me what's going on," she said. She'd been my friend long enough to know it was about my mother, of course.

I explained. Same old story. An argument over some imagined attack I'd made on Mom's "reputation," then her ripping my self-esteem to shreds, and ending up with her getting physically violent. Now, my mom is petite, at least 6 inches shorter, but I just... let her do it, because I couldn't imagine really defying her. So I ran away. Again.

But this time, talking it over with Shanna, I was reminded that I'd run away to Shanna's before... oh, about twenty years ago. And I thought to myself, "Am I going to be doing this twenty years from now, too?"

The thought just stopped me cold.

I shrugged and cut off discussion. "You've heard all this before anyway," I said. Shanna gave me a hug, told me to raid her closet in the morning and made a joke about it being good luck we wore the same shoe size.

The next morning, I didn't go home. Instead, I called up a real estate agent and started apartment hunting.

That was six years ago. I never ran back. But after a few weeks, I tried calling Mom. Nothing but incoherent accusations and threats, so I hung up. A week later, she got my new number from the phone book, and called me. We chatted for a few minutes, and that was the beginning.

Things are not perfect, not by a long shot. But she realizes now that she doesn't hold all the cards. She can't force me to go along with whatever she wants, period. Not with threats, not with insults, not with anything. If she wants to have a relationship with me, it has to be one of mutual respect, or there won't be one at all.

Now that she understands that, she does try, so much more than she used to... sometimes she reverts, and it hurts, but I stick by my boundaries. She comes around again. And I feel like, for the first time, I'm actually getting to know her. I don't know if I'll ever feel like she's a "good mother," but I'm starting to feel like she really does care, that she can and that I can care for her. Because I want to, not because she makes me.

-Lauren P.

Lauren's story is an inspiring one. Many who have suffered under the controlling authority of a borderline personality return to that abuser time and time again, just as Lauren did. Despite being able to run away in the heat of the moment, they lack sufficient perspective to resist returning.

Lauren's sudden strength came from her sudden shift in perspective. She realized, when she remembered the incident from twenty years past that nothing was changing, and that unless she herself changed, nothing *would.*

Chapter 4
Isolation: Why it's Dangerous, How it Happens

Your mother may have directly or indirectly contributed to your being or feeling incredibly isolated. Some BPs do not have the intention to isolate or entrap their loved ones. But driven by paranoia, the obsessive desire to control situations, and their irrational fears and self-absorbed insecurities, they give into behaviors that result in manipulation that ends in isolation. And unfortunately, in some cases, there *is* a deliberate attempt to control loved ones through isolation.

Being Isolated Isn't an Option

If you are in a climate of isolation, it must be immediately addressed. Why? Isolation itself has profoundly harmful effects on the both the human psyche *and* the human body. Social isolation can dramatically undermine your taking further steps to improve your own self-esteem, confidence, and quality of life, let alone any goals you have regarding the improvement of the interactions between you and your mother.

Resolving the issue of social isolation is critical for numerous reasons, some having to do with your health and well-being in a general sense and some having a more specific impact on the relationship you have with your mother.

You don't just deserve to have a support network. Human beings *need* social interaction to be happy and healthy. Social interaction fulfills many of our needs and lends us strength in many different ways.

Healthy social interaction will also contribute to your healing from the wounds to your psyche inflicted by your mother—even those wounds which don't seem related to the topic of isolation at all. Part of the reason we interact with other people is to build on the way we see the world. Having a well-rounded worldview helps us heal from things that harm us, especially psychologically, because having perspective on the situation gives us the tools we need to move forward.

Perspective is a large concept with a lot of different meanings. When we discuss it generally, we usually mean something synonymous with objectivity. To see something in perspective is to see it objectively. Having friends and confidants helps us do this when we can have our preconceptions challenged in a respectful and supportive way.

Perspective and Reality

In art, perspective is a term for the technique of representing something accurately, creating the illusion of three dimensions in a drawing, of representing the size and mass of an object relative to the sizes and mass of the other objects in view in such a way to support that illusion. There are two types of methods used. One is usually referred to as "one-point perspective," and the other as "two-point perspective."

They're referred to in this way because the "perspective" is obtained in each case by depending on either "one" or "two" established and unchanging "vanishing points."

When you stand in the center of a flat, straight, empty road, facing down it, the lines of the side of the road seem to eventually meet, to converge, with the center line. The point at which the lines converge is the vanishing point. This is one point-perspective.

Although we know that the sides of the road run parallel to one another, the illusion is very convincing isn't it? One-point perspective is very dramatic, but extremely limiting for the artist. Only under very rigid, controlled circumstances can certain things be portrayed with any accuracy using this method. It dictates the point of view very strictly, and the subject matter choices are restricted to a few things that lend themselves well to it.

> *I guess it just finally seemed like her reality was just... the one I had to learn to live in. Not that it was right, I mean, I knew things were messed up. But it still seemed like her way was the only choice. I knew it was awful, but she just kinda drowned out everything else.*

This is what it's like when you are isolated and rescind your right to have a personal perspective on events and situations, when you submit to her perspective, her perceptions, in every circumstance. Even if you may still understand, on one level, that things are not the way they should be, it becomes increasingly difficult to imagine them to be any *other* way. Solutions seem completely out of reach. There is only one ultimate conclusion: the one your mother chooses. There is only one destination—hers—and there is no conceivable deviation from the course she choose to take to reach that destination. Your very ability to interact with reality in becomes limited, because your mother has demanded that you accept *her* reality and that reality may bear very little resemblance to the world as it truly is.

Two-point perspective makes use of two vanishing points. When you stand facing the corner of a rectangular building, the walls on each side seem to get shorter as your eye moves from the corner you're facing. The larger the building is, the greater this gradual change appears to be. If the building were large enough, the top and bottom lines that define the walls would converge in the same way the sides of the road do in one point perspective.

> *Me against her. Her against me. Seems like that was every situation, everything, all the time. There was so much conflict. Nothing could ever be resolved because she couldn't budge an inch. It didn't matter how much I tried to get her to see my point of view... or ANY point of view, other than her crazy, paranoid one.*

When you're isolated from friends and family, from a support network, but attempt to maintain your own opinions in your relationship, it's a lot like two point perspective. It's an improvement over one-point perspective but it is by no means ideal. Two-point perspective can show us two sides of a building, or two sides of a situation, but it doesn't allow us to walk around the building. It doesn't allow us to see the *entirety* of what is happening in the picture.

We Need Outside Relationships for Perspective

Artists study one point perspective and two point perspective in order to understand the mechanics of illusion. But at some point, they learn to utilize more than the limiting vanishing points these methods offer. Real life is much more complex than a picture. Real situations can't be defined with vanishing points. Real roads don't go on straight and flat into eternity until they converge on themselves. And real relationships can't follow the rigid rules of one person's point of view.

You know already how terrifying a lack of realistic perspective is. You've seen the results of that in your mother's behavior, in her out of proportion reactions to events, in her reactions to completely *imagined* events.

We live in communities for psychological reasons, not just material ones. Communities and relationships provide balance, perspective, and help us overcome our own individual limitations. You may have accepted or even chosen your isolation as a form of sacrifice to "help" your mother in the past, but that must change. You can't help her if you're trapped in a rigid, inflexible, unchanging world, whether it's one she's created herself or one the two of you create together.

It's not that having friends or family means they'll tell you how to "fix" things, it's that without interaction and healthy support, without other, healthy relationships in your life, you have no basis for comparison, no way to even identify what needs to be fixed to begin with.

We Need Outside Relationships for Emotional Support

We all need support and caring from others. More specifically, we all need *healthy, respectful* support and caring from others. No one can be "everything" for someone else, which is why we should have a variety of strong, healthy, unique relationships in our lives.

Even if your mother was capable of providing love and emotional support in a healthy, respectful way, you'd *still* need other people in your life.

Perspective and Emotional Support are *not* Luxuries, They're Necessities

Having relationships in our lives that are mutually beneficial is not a treat or a luxury. Having coffee with a friend once a week, or being able to chit chat on the phone with your brother, or going away for a few days vacation with friends now and then are essential for your well-being, which itself is a crucial factor in having a healthier relationship with your mother. Giving them up is not a noble sacrifice, or a concession to her illness. Giving them up is tantamount to giving up food, or water, or air.

How Does Isolation Happen?

It's sad... I ran into John the other day. We were best friends forever. He was happy to see me, and it did my heart good to see him.

He asked, "Where have you been, stranger?! What have you been up to?"

I kind of laughed and said, "Oh, nothing really. I haven't been anywhere. Same old same old."

He looked confused, and replied, "No, seriously? I thought for sure you must have moved away. I mean no one has even seen you in ages."

I guess the truth is I didn't move farther away, I moved farther in... farther into her world, her needs, her fears.

It often happens so gradually that we don't realize it until we find ourselves isolated and apparently friendless.

It happens when you turn off your cell once Mom gets home, to avoid her pouting if you take a call. It happens when you turn down a lunch date with friends because Mom accuses you of talking about her behind her back to them. It happens when you don't visit Dad on holidays, because since the divorce, Mom throws tantrums or breaks down if she hears that you've been in contact with him.

It happens when you turn down so many friends so often that they just assume you'll say no, so they don't call. It happens when stop inviting people over because you're embarrassed about the situation at home, about the rules you have to follow, or because you're afraid your mother will make a huge scene in front of them.

It happens when all of these things add up until it seems like the only person in your life is her.

Chapter 5
Combating Isolation: The Basics

You can't cure her of her disorder. But you can take steps to protect yourself from the most devastating effects of it by setting boundaries. Much of the pain and terror that she's visited on you through her disorder have been the result of her disregarding the boundaries that you, like all human beings, deserve to have. She has ignored the limits she should have imposed on her own words and actions to avoid hurting you.

Setting and enforcing boundaries is the best and most effective way of coping with a borderline personality. She won't acknowledge boundaries that are not completely and clearly explained, without room for negotiation, and she won't respect boundaries if disrespecting them carries no consequence.

Think Through the Causes for Your Isolation

How exactly have you become isolated? Is it through guilt trips? Does she go into a rage when you interact with others? Does she create scenes when you have a guest?

Before discussing it with her, identify the actions she uses and the things she says that most directly contribute to your isolation. Those that are unacceptable behavior from one respective adult to another are the ones that need to be addressed with boundaries.

Setting and Enforcing Boundaries that Protect Your Interactions with Others

Sit down with her when you are both calm and explain the boundary you'd like to set. Describe the behavior that is causing the problem. Tell her what is unacceptable about it and explain what would be an appropriate way to express herself.

The most vital ways to enforce boundaries revolve around first, not allowing her tantrum to have the desired effect, and second, disengaging from her immediately when she tries to challenge the boundary. Enforcing boundaries has nothing to do with arguing or "making her stop." You can't make her do anything; you can't control her.

But you can control how you react to her.

Do Not Reward Inappropriate Behavior

Explain to her that when she crosses the boundary, it will not have the effect she desires. If she causes a scene when you have a guest, you will not be embarrassed or ashamed and ask them to leave. Instead, you and your guest will leave, and conclude your visit pleasantly, without further disruption from her.

If she destroys your belongings as retaliation when you visit your aunt, tell her that will not prevent you from spending time with your family. If you must, you'll put a lock on the door to your room so that she can't enter it when you aren't there.

Disengaging

Do not give her attention in return for her behavior. If she verbally attacks you for talking on the phone, explain that when that happens, you will go elsewhere to make your phone calls. If she begins demonizing or making accusations against your friends, walk out of the room. Refuse to discuss the situation with her until she can do so without resorting to the things that cross the boundaries you've set.

Setting Your Own Goals

If you've become isolated already, being socially interactive and building relationships will depend on more than just dealing with her behaviors. Isolation perpetuates itself. It's not easy to rebuild contacts with friends and family once you've become accustomed to an isolated existence.

Make a list of people you'd like to get back into contact with. Set goals for yourself to give them a call, set up a coffee date, etc. Although dealing with your mother may be exhausting and leave you wanting to cancel extra activities, don't give in to that type of self-defeating mentality.

You may even feel some social anxiety when you begin socializing again. That's completely normal and the best cure for it is to keep socializing.

Chapter 6
Verbal and Physical Abuse: Why it Must Stop

It's almost inevitable for a borderline personality to eventually cross the line from "difficult to deal with" to "abusive." When the BP is in a position of power or authority over another person, just as a mother is in a position of power and authority over her child, it *is* inevitable. With power over someone else comes the obligation to be gentle, to respect their boundaries even when they cannot defend them, to teach respect by example.

BPs are chronically insecure, and feel the need for excessive amounts of control to compensate for that. No matter how secure their position may be in reality, they perceive themselves as being surrounded by threats. Threats to their sanity, threats to their identity, threats to their emotions, threats to those they love.

In desperate situations, we all have a tendency to take desperate measures. The problem is that to the borderline personality, *all* situations—or nearly all—are desperate. Thanks to their over-reactions and "preventative" measures, behavior which would be understandable only in the most extreme situations becomes increasingly frequent and triggered by events of decreasing importance. At times there may be no perceptible cause whatsoever.

Abuse has a Cumulative Effect

Regardless of your age now, or how long you have coped with her abuse, it must stop, immediately. You cannot continue a relationship with her if her behavior consistently crosses the line into abuse.

Staying in contact with your mother may be your goal, but safety absolutely must be your first priority. If you cannot put your safety first—if you cannot come to terms with the idea that you do not deserve and should not tolerate being abused—you must cut off contact while you do.

As long as you accept abuse, no matter what your reasons are, and as long as she refuses to alter her behavior when you set boundaries, the relationship can and will only worsen and become more dangerous.

This is not simply a matter of physical safety, either. The longer you tolerate abuse, even if you feel confident that you are identifying it as such, the less able you will be to set any other sort of boundaries or limits with her. Over time your ability to understand personal boundaries in any context has eroded; tolerance of abuse exacerbates this and destroys your confidence.

Nor does this apply only to the relationship between you and her. Eventually (if it hasn't already) your lack of boundaries and injured self confidence will impact your life in many other ways, and in every relationship you have.

If you have labored in this relationship under the idea that it is your obligation to help her, it bears repeating that you cannot do that while you yourself are being systematically attacked by her behaviors. You must be well yourself in order to help anyone else.

Understanding Why Your Mother is Abusive

Unlike traditional abusers, it's rare for borderline personalities to consciously manipulate those they're abusing. They truly believe they are behaving in an appropriate manner. Even when they recognize that the behaviors are out of line, they are unable to self-regulate.

It's urgently important for you to understand this. Not because it functions as an "excuse" for the way your mother treats you—whatever her intentions, the results remain the same and the behavior must not be tolerated. Rather, it's important to understand this for you own mental health.

Even if you know the abuse is wrong, and can identify it, it's incredibly difficult not to take it personally. Especially when the attacks are, inevitably, personal attacks, and from someone who knows you so well. Your anger and pain are justified.

Nonetheless learning to detach from the abuse—to not take it personally—is of utmost importance. When you are able to understand and truly integrate the idea that your mother is reacting to triggers and perceived (even if fictitious) threats and *not* to *you,* your understanding will help you deal with the emotional effects of the abuse.

Why? Because when you take her actions personally, you do two things. One, you implicitly accept that you are the *cause* of the abuse. Two, you deepen the wound inflicted upon yourself.

Not taking it personally doesn't mean not being hurt by it. It's natural to be hurt by hurtful words and actions. But when you absorb the abuse as being personal, when you believe you are the "cause," it's as if you take the knife from her hand and deepen the cut.

Cause and Effect

The causes of abusive behaviors are always difficult to understand. When the abuser is a mother with borderline personality disorder, what was murky becomes seemingly impenetrable.

Part of this is due to her own twisted perspectives and interpretations of reality. She is prone to overreactions to mundane occurrences; the thoughts that precede these reactions can be so paranoid that they qualify as delusional. She is in deep denial regarding her own culpability due to her self-absorption. In truth, the most frequent "cause" behind her actions is her own mental illness, not surrounding events or people.

Another reason the causes of her actions are difficult to deduce is that she may be intentionally engaging in deception or misdirection. While her deceptions may or may not be conscious, a borderline personality is geared towards defending her true thoughts and feelings against any "prying" inquiry. She knows, deep down, that her version of reality is fragile, that her paranoia and accusations may not hold up to the light of day. She may justify this to herself with layer upon layer of further paranoia, which only confuses the issue more.

This is not necessarily because she does not trust you, or because she intends to trick you. On the contrary, she may believe it is best for everyone involved not to know her true thoughts and feelings. She wants to protect herself, yes, but she also may have the misguided belief that she is protecting others.

Many BPs recognize that they are unwell, and consider their thoughts and feelings to be poisonous or toxic. The fact that the things they say and do to hide these toxic thoughts, feelings, and beliefs are in reality more harmful to others than their true feelings is a point of logic that escapes them.

While you cannot read her mind, and cannot trust that the words she speaks are a true representation of her inner thoughts, there are other ways to find the catalysts for her abusive behaviors.

The cause may be her sickness, but the direct link between the environment and her actions can be referred to as a trigger. Your actions may indeed "trigger" abuse even if they are entirely benign. Learning the difference between what is a trigger and what is a cause is important because it helps to free you from misplaced guilt, which itself is crippling and a tool of abuse.

A trigger is anything that causes us to react—whether or not the reaction is warranted. A cause is that which is actually *responsible* for the result.

For example, she may fly into a rage or sink into a depression when you visit your father. But visiting your father is *not* the cause. Ultimately the cause of her actions in this case is insecurity and the intensity with which BPs blow things out of proportion—or themselves take personally events which have nothing to do with them.

The event which triggers the resulting abusive or self-harming behavior is not a source of blame for anyone involved. Even if visiting your father is a trigger, that does not mean you should not visit your father.

What it does give you is a clue to what the actual cause is, and further understanding her actual motives can help you see more clearly that *you* are not the cause of her actions, and that you do *not* deserve blame, abuse, or guilt trips.

Chapter 7
Combating Abuse: Basic First Steps

Safety

Before you can begin to identify triggering situations or explore ways to defuse them, however, you must already be in a position of safety and security personally. Unless you and she are able to work on your relationship in an atmosphere free of terror, no lasting improvement can be made.

The boundaries and defensive strategies we'll discuss in this chapter will help to create a safer environment. As with any boundaries, you must be able to set them and enforce them, and she must have some willingness to cooperate.

Strongly consider setting a boundary that dictates that a third party—one you trust—must be present whenever you see her. It may influence her behavior in a positive manner, and even if it does not, you have a reliable witness to the way she treats you.

Zero Tolerance Policy

Whether or not a boundary for an abusive behavior has been set yet or not, you *must not* tolerate any behavior that compromises your safety. When she engages in abusive actions, your enforcement of your boundaries must be swift and decisive. This is vital, both for your own personal safety and if you have any hope of the relationship being salvageable.

Explain, in a quiet, reasonable way that, regardless of how much you care about her, you cannot and will not allow her to abuse you. You cannot help her or support her if you are being abused. Tell her that if the abuse continues you will not continue being in contact with her because it can only hurt you and will not help her in any way.

You have no obligation to stay in or return to any abusive situation, no matter what your relationship is to the abuser or how ill the abuser may be.

Firmly Believe You Don't Deserve to be Abused

You need to do some personal reflection, too. Being abused has profound effects on your psyche. Understanding and truly *believing* that you do not deserve to be abused and will not tolerate abusive behavior may be harder than it sounds. If your mother has been abusive, seeking professional help with coping with the psychological and emotional fallout is strongly recommended. Just because she's the one with a "disorder" doesn't mean you don't deserve help, too.

Set some rules for your own actions apart from boundaries related to her behavior. For example, not keeping her abusive behavior a secret anymore, not covering up her abuse of yourself or others, or admitting to yourself that certain things she does are abusive even if in the past you have let them slide.

Setting Boundaries for Safety

Enforcing boundaries that concern your immediate safety has as much to do with enforcing your own behavior as hers. You may have fallen into a pattern of allowing or enabling her abuse. Abusive situations warp our perceptions and lead to helplessness and despair. You *must* overcome this to care for yourself.

If Boundaries Aren't Enough

No matter how diligent you are about your boundaries or how much progress you make emotionally and psychologically yourself, she may continue to be abusive. This isn't your fault. You can only control your half of the relationship. Don't blame yourself for her actions. If she cannot or will not stop being abusive, your only option is to cut off contact with her completely.

Chapter 8
Cutting off Contact

Despite your best efforts, your compassion, your firmness, and your intentions, she may continue to disrespect your boundaries. It may be an obvious matter of personal safety—she is continuing to be abusive, for example. It may be a less easily quantifiable situation; you may simply realize that you cannot go on in the relationship as it stands and expect improvement.

We all have limits to what we can do. We may say or believe that we can or will do anything for those we love, but that isn't true of *anyone*. The fact is that those we love, who love us in return, respect our limits if they are emotionally and psychologically healthy.

Most of the people we love do not force us to our limits, and beyond, to a breaking point. Your mother, however, as a borderline personality, probably cannot sense your limits, and if she can—she feels so threatened by them that she *intends* to push you past them. It's a sort of self-fulfilling prophesy: "Everyone abandons me, so I will prove my son or daughter wrong, when he or she denies the intention to abandon me."

You cannot stop her from forcing the situation out of control if she is determined to do it. Borderline personality disorder is a serious illness, but those who suffer from it *do have free will.*

And even if the reason for the situation is not her choice, that doesn't mean you should stay. Staying in a situation that is harming you, that you can't keep contained, is not going to help anyone. Not even her. All it will do is reinforce her unhealthy behaviors.

Leaving or cutting off contact is not "the easy way out," but it may be the *only* way. She is very likely to resist it, and even more likely to increase the intensity and frequency of her unhealthy behaviors in response.

Preparation

If you are in a situation that represents immediate physical danger to yourself, you will have less (if any) time for preparation. If this is the case, you will have to execute a very decisive and complete break in contact, and may need to involve law enforcement and other professional agencies. If you live with her, you need to contact a domestic abuse hotline and find out your immediate local options for shelter and support.

If, however, you have some time, there are things you can do that may make the break more successful and less stressful.

While Still in Contact

While you may be most motivated to leave when things are dramatically out of control, it is best to leave the situation as calmly as possible. This means that while you are setting up your preparations for leaving or cutting off contact you do what you can to allow the situation to be as low key as possible.

Making threats to leave will *not* accomplish that. But cutting off contact without warning will also result in greater drama. The middle ground may be difficult to find. Basically it consists of neither accepting nor opposing your mother's behaviors.

Whether it's rage, declarations of love, or tearful sadness, try to keep your reactions as calm and non-committal as you can. At this point your goal is not to solve or improve anything. You just want to calm things down very temporarily. These measures wouldn't work in the long term, but they can provide some help over the short term.

While you are preparing yourself, mentally, emotionally, and strategically, for the break, do give her some indication that it is coming. Not threats, and not necessarily "hints" but calmly stating that things are not working. Go beyond "calm" into *boring*.

You well know that intensity and excitement, whether positive or negative, tend to affect her behaviors exponentially. She is likely to find a source of drama and intensity even in your calmest, least extravagant statements; don't give her any extra fuel.

Building a Support Network

If you live with your mother, this is obviously going to be key. But even if you live separately, it's very important.

Without a support network that is aware of the situation *before* you leave or break contact, it is going to be extremely difficult to stick with your decision.

It's also very likely that she will twist the reality—you leaving/breaking off contact because she is hurtful and you've done everything you can to no avail—into something else. Borderline personalities often lie or misrepresent situations to others in order to gain sympathy or support for their actions.

Consider the friends and family that will be supportive of your decision and who will be able to support you in safely and effectively sticking with it, especially those that already have some understanding of your mother's issues. Talk to them *before* you cut off contact. Let them know it is coming. Let them know you believe she will react badly. Explain that it is not a decision being made in the heat of the moment, but one which despite its difficulty is necessary.

This does several things. One, it gives you much needed emotional support. It affirms your decision. It provides you with perspective when you second guess yourself or when she makes you feel guilty for one reason or another.

Your support network will be there to remind you of your calm, rational, and justifiable reasons for ending contact, when that happens.

It also provides something of a countermeasure against her unrealistic beliefs. In her distress, she may even outright lie or attempt to deceive others about what is going on. She may make false accusations or she may misinterpret and misrepresent actual events.

When you prepare by speaking to those you trust to support you before that happens, you have done something to protect both them and yourself from her lies. If they understand that this is a planned decision, her sudden announcement that she threw you out because *you* were abusive, or hurtful, etc. will carry no weight.

And it helps to protect you from her actually convincing you of your fault. When she realizes you are ceasing contact with her, she will attempt to place guilt and blame on you. Her sincerity, whether it's real or not, in her belief that you are the one at fault can be very convincing, especially when you are distressed yourself. Your loved ones can remind you that when you calm you understood things far more clearly.

Making a Clean Break

If she has so far demonstrated that she cannot or will not respect your boundaries and limitations, this must be a clean break. She will not respond favorably to your backing down and allowing some contact if she pressures you. To her, that will indicate that pressuring you *works* and it will only reinforce the very situation that led to this outcome.

You may in fact have hope that contact can resume at some point but this is not something you can express to her. Remember that she thinks in black and white terms. Either there is no contact or she will believe that with enough pressure she can behave in any way towards you.

Do not use words or phrases like, "for now," "maybe later," "at some point." You don't have to say this is "forever" (unless it is), but at most just reiterate calmly that you cannot be in contact with her. Period. Not "I can't be in contact with you right now," or "while things are this way," etc. Be absolutely and completely clear that all contact is stopping.

If you do hope or want contact to resume at some point, you need to be firm with yourself also. Set a time limit which must pass without her pressuring or trying to contact you. Do *not* tell her this timeline. Do not even hint that there is such a thing.

Consider the conditions that must be met before you allow *yourself* to resume contact.

For example:

–Three months must pass without any contact or attempts on her part to contact
–You fulfill a personal goal of seeking therapy for yourself
–You discuss the decision with your therapist before making contact again
–You feel confident about your ability to resume contact with healthy boundaries

Your list may be different, but you should make one while your understanding of why you cut off contact is still fresh in your mind.

Grieving and Guilt

Although the decision to end contact was yours, it's natural and understandable to feel sad, even to miss her. It's natural not to, also. In neither case should you be angry with yourself.

You should not feel guilty to be relieved or happy to be free of her influence. It doesn't make you a bad person or a heartless one. Feeling proud of yourself for making a difficult decision is justified; feeling liberated is justified.

Nor should you be angry with yourself for grieving over the relationship. Regardless of her behavior or her illness, it's entirely natural to have a very strong attachment to her. It's natural to still love her and feel concern. While you may have chosen to cut off communication, you did not choose the circumstances which made it *necessary.*

Chapter 9
Boundaries in Depth

The intention of this book is to provide you with the most important information and tools to protect yourself from the ravages of having a borderline mother. It by no means encompasses everything there is to say on the matter.

Before you can do more, your safety must be a priority, which is why we have chosen to focus on the topics chosen here. If the boundaries and measures already discussed can be achieved, you can work on the relationship further with the potential for some success.

The building blocks of having a fruitful relationship with your mother will always be boundaries. This is in part because of the fact that borderline personalities in general do not have the ability to discern or respect boundaries without having them spelled out and enforced, and in part because of the particular nature of the mother child relationship.

As human beings we grow into having boundaries. Our parents set our boundaries when we are tiny; they ideally respect boundaries we didn't even know we should have. We learn our boundaries and our expectations of how others should behave towards us from our parents.

Obviously your situation is different. While many mothers may tend to take advantage of their motherhood to challenge our boundaries—being nosey about our lives, or teasing us with good intention—the BP mother doesn't just take advantage, she obliterates boundaries. Her emotions roll over them like tanks.

She didn't teach you appropriate boundaries to begin with, which has left you at a disadvantage. Even people with a healthy understanding of boundaries, however, can fall prey to BPs. It's not normally necessary to *need* to enforce rigid boundaries with other emotionally secure adults, after all.

We are used to having a certain understanding of other people's limitations and the expectation that they will respect our own without having to explicitly state them, let alone enforce them with prearranged consequences. That expectation gets us nowhere with borderline personality disordered persons, however. And in the case of mothers with BPD, the situation is even more extreme.

You are uncertain *yourself* about what boundaries should be, having been constantly exposed to someone who should have been teaching you about them but instead was constantly tearing them down. She not only does not comprehend that others' boundaries (if she even realizes they exist) are more important than her acting out her feelings and urges, but has had a lifetime habit of ignoring and disabling yours.

What are Boundaries?

Boundaries are exactly what a BP needs and exactly what she doesn't have. They're the rules we set for ourselves about what is and is not appropriate, respectful behavior. They apply both to us and to others. Boundaries are what help us each to separate our impulses from the actions we actually carry out or the words we actually say. In your relationship with your mother, you may actually have boundaries—bad ones.

For example, when you go along with her behavior even when it is out-of-line, you are obeying a sort of boundary. At some point you have been taught, or decided, that the impulse to reject harmful behavior must be reined in.

Positive boundaries are things like "Even when I am angry, I don't call people names." Or, "Even when I have a bad day, it's not okay to be hurtful to someone else." Typically we set boundaries without thinking about it, and we tend to set more boundaries for our own behavior than for others. It is not usually necessary to tell mature adults, "It's inappropriate for you to scream obscenities at me," because it's more or less common knowledge.

With your mother, however, you cannot assume that she will set any boundaries on her own behavior.

Why They're Important

Boundaries are more than just helpful. They do more than make interacting more pleasant. They're *crucial* for society and relationships.

If we're all so calm and rational, why are boundaries so important?

Well, we *aren't*—any of us—all that calm and rational. Borderline personalities lack control, and they experience things in heightened intensity, but their emotions are not different from anyone else's. We have boundaries because we have the same impulses to cause a scene or call someone names or be mean because we had a bad day.

Impulses may be powerful and sincere enough in the fact that they are real urges, but being secure and mentally healthy means being aware that they are *only* impulses. When things calm down and the impulse has passed, we feel differently. Even while having the impulse to yell at someone or blame them for our bad day, we may realize on some level it's not going to help and it isn't really their fault.

Our own boundaries—those we don't allow others to cross—also protect our sense of self. Our boundaries define both an area of responsibility and an area of safety and security. We are responsible for our own actions and how they affect others, and we are also entitled to personal space and having others respect us through controlling their impulses.

Boundaries are not Selfish

Your mother may imply or outright state that your boundaries are driven by selfishness. You will at some point question whether or not this is actually true. She can be very convincing of her own defenselessness, her own freedom from blame.

Furthermore, even mentally sound people give in to their impulses in extreme situations. For example, if someone's pet runs out in front of a car unexpectedly and gets hit, the owner may scream at the driver, call him names, even threaten violence, because of the intensity of her emotional reaction. Even if the driver is not at fault, he is likely to understand that she is not reacting to him or actually blaming him. But we're able to make these types of exceptions only if we are able to distinguish whether or not a situation is extreme enough to warrant it.

To a BP, any and every situation may "justify" their behavior. In fact, if they have feelings and impulses not related to any actual events or people, they may fabricate or precipitate an "extreme" situation *in order* to act out their impulses.

This is why it is not selfish to be very firm about enforcing your boundaries. It is, in fact, destructive to all involved if you *don't.*

Many borderline personalities actually discover some of the security they themselves crave when their loved ones set and enforce boundaries. Because they frequently feel as much remorse for their impulsive reactions as they do the drive to carry them out, it is a relief to have someone else tell them they must stop.

Confidence in Boundaries

Setting boundaries is different than simply announcing that a behavior is unacceptable when it happens and insisting it end. While you shouldn't allow her to believe that you accept inappropriate behavior, that itself is not setting a boundary.

Confidence is an important element here. This includes your confidence in the fact that setting the boundary is the right thing to do, your continued confidence in enforcing it, and *her* confidence in understanding what the boundary means.

The first hurdle with setting a boundary will typically be her belief that, regardless of what you say, the boundary actually represents you abandoning her, you not loving her, you attacking her feelings, you invalidating her. This hurdle will not be overcome simply by calmly and logically explaining it, but that is still the first step you must take.

Repeatedly enforcing the boundary, however, and positive reinforcement when boundaries are respected, can give her confidence that the boundary does indeed mean what you *say* it means. Stated and enforced boundaries may initially be taken as a sign of distrust, and indeed in one sense they are. You know from experience that you cannot trust in her ability to regulate her actions. But having boundaries doesn't perpetuate distrust. It actually builds trust over time, for both of you.

Setting Boundaries

As mentioned before, boundaries should always be "set" in a very explicit, straightforward manner. Setting boundaries should be done when you are both calm and in as good a frame of mind as possible. If there's an episode that illustrates to you the need for a new boundary, it's fine to express that at the time, but you still need to sit down with her later and spell it out when things are calmer.

Think through the boundary you want to set thoroughly before you have the conversation with her about it. Have a very clear idea, yourself, of what the boundary is, and how you will enforce it. Think about how you will encourage her, as well, when she does respect it.

This is important because while having the conversation with her, you cannot allow her to think that the boundary is some sort of negotiation. It must be very clear that you are not there to *ask* her for the right to set the boundary, and that you will not argue about it. It's not a debate. That doesn't mean you won't hear her out, and respect her feelings, and explain the real reasons for it, but don't defend yourself, or defend your choice. It's not something that needs to be defended; it's simply *how it has to be.* Utilize the validating and explaining techniques described below when she becomes distressed or

Enforcing Boundaries

Explain to her that you're not trying to control her. Your boundaries and enforcing them is not about controlling her emotions or her freedom. Instead, it's a way of explaining to her *your* actions and *your* reactions in response.

For example, one of your boundaries might be that you will not continue a conversation if she is insulting or demeaning you. Explain as clearly as you can what that constitutes. Name calling, screaming, accusing you of things that are patently untrue or unfair, for example.

Then calmly state what your reaction will be and why. In this case, leaving the room or the house, cutting off the conversation, until she calms down, would be a good response.

Reiterate that it is not a punishment, but a proactive stance you are taking to improve your relationship with one another and to maintain your own self respect. Explain that it is something you are doing to help yourself in a healthy way, not to harm her. And continue to be clear that it is not her emotions you are reacting to but her *actions.* You care about her feelings, but there are limits to the types of actions you can tolerate.

When she crosses an established boundary, you must carry out the discussed enforcement *every time.* If you give in because she is being more out of control than usual, she will only see that as illustrating that she can "make you understand" with increasingly inappropriate actions.

Validating and Explaining

As already discussed, learning to validate her feelings without agreeing with her perceptions of a situation can help. Her feelings are, after all, very real. Her fears are overblown or misplaced or based on paranoid ideation, but she is really feeling them. Her anger is very real, even when it is not being expressed appropriately.

Validation is accomplished by saying simply that you recognize her feeling, that you understand that she is in distress. You shouldn't apologize for it, because it isn't your fault (even if she is triggered by something relating to you). BPs sometimes behave dramatically because they want to *show* how intense their emotions are. If that's the case with your mother, then validating her and letting her know that you already understand she is having very intense feelings may help mitigate her impulse to act them out in inappropriate ways.

Validation is most important when your mother is emotional, yet it is the most challenging time to communicate with her.

Acknowledge without Agreeing

You endeavor to keep yourself calm. Before disagreeing or defending yourself (both of which BPs have a strong tendency to interpret as being reprimanded for their emotions), acknowledge her feelings, that they are real, and that they matter to you.

Explore the Reasons for Her Reaction

Ask for information about *why* she is reacting this way, and what she is actually feeling. How much you will be able to get will largely depend on her ability to communicate effectively considering the situation. Encourage her to elaborate by asking questions.

Confirm That You Care About Her Feelings

As she answers your questions, continue to acknowledge her feelings and your concern

Present Your Interpretation

Do your best to do this without defending yourself or becoming defensive. First of all, you don't need to defend yourself when you haven't done anything wrong. Secondly, she will perceive defensive language as you attacking her—hard to believe, when she is the one attacking, but nonetheless likely. Try to state the actual situation in as objective and detached way as possible.

Example of Validating and Explaining:

Susan- *Mother with Borderline Personality disorder*
Robin- *Susan's Adult Daughter*

Susan: Why did you call me? What do you want? I know you don't actually care so you must want something.

Robin: (startled) What? Mom, what's wrong?
Susan: You have some nerve asking that! How could I not be angry about what you've done?!

83

Robin:	Mom, wow, I can tell you're really upset. I don't really know what it is I did, though, can you please explain?
Susan:	I saw your car over at your brother's house. You know he and I aren't talking. I know you were over there listening to his lies about me.
Robin:	I'd be really mad if someone did that to me, too, Mom. I understand that you're really hurt. I went over because he invited me for dinner. It wasn't intended to hurt your feelings.

Patience and Realistic Expectations

Boundaries and validation will not "cure" her of borderline personality disorder. Nor will it solve any problems immediately. It may take a considerable amount of time before you see results on her part at all. At the very least, this routine should help prevent bad situations from escalating.

Ideally, and if she is also making an effort, several things can happen if you are consistent at validating and then explaining.

First, you may notice she is better able to clarify what she is thinking and feeling when elaborating, even if her reactions are out of proportion. Her reactive feelings and thoughts themselves are likely to remain overly intense and distinctly paranoid, as a function of the disorder, but she may eventually learn to express them without overt blaming and attacks.

The most important aspect of boundaries and validation routines are not what they do for her, but for you. Boundaries help you preserve yourself and defend yourself against hurtful actions. They help you build self-confidence. Validating and explaining help you take a step back and understand more fully that her actions are not your *fault*.

All of these things also help you to gain self control. You didn't have a good example of mature, self-regulation from her. Self control isn't just not yelling and screaming. It's also about maintaining a clear, realistic outlook in stressful situations. When you don't allow yourself to get drawn into her world, when you don't allow her to force you to defend yourself when you didn't do anything wrong, you are practicing self control.

In the end, how much these things help her is *up* to her. But they *will* help you.

Jonathon's Story

Sometimes I don't really know whether my mother's behavior is really my fault or not.

If it *is* my fault, then it's not really fair for me to punish her with a "boundary," right? It makes sense enough on paper, yes. But once we have some kind of disagreement, things get out of control *so fast*, and...

Well, I've said and done some in appropriate things myself. And that usually leads to her really freaking out on me, and threatening suicide, or accusing me of crazy stuff, or saying she's going to tell lies about me to my father or my wife and kids.

I don't know. I just know that by the point where she does something really out of line, I feel like *I've* crossed the line. I mean, nowhere near the type of stuff she does, but still. And I just end up doing whatever it takes to calm her down, because she wouldn't have gotten *so* upset if I'd had some self control.

-Jonathon L.

Jonathon is expressing a very common insecurity for an adult child of a BP mother to experience. It is a natural result of being raised by a borderline personality, but through new experiences and new priorities, this insecurity can be addressed.

Once things get "out of control," it suddenly seems much less clear who is crossing whose boundaries. All adults may have the tendency to behave more as children do, when confronted with their parents. This is true whether or not one's mother is a borderline personality.

When Jonathon's mother loses control, he probably feels a loss of control, himself. What is encouraging about Jonathon's letter is his recognition of this tendency.

Part of losing control, of course, is crossing boundaries. She says something hurtful, and he responds with something hurtful. Everyone has the potential to "lose control" when pushed far enough. But a borderline personality may perceive others as pushing her around when no such thing is happening.

She feels pushed, so she pushes back. Her actions, of course, have a very real effect upon her son. Later, Jonathon looks back and says to himself, "My behavior was no better than hers, in the end. Who am I to impose these boundaries, when I can't respect boundaries myself?"

The problem isn't that Jonathon doesn't "deserve" to impose boundaries. On the contrary, this type of situation probably occurs because Jonathon's boundaries aren't well defined, or have only been defined for "worst case scenarios."

What does that mean? Perhaps Jonathon has assumed that he doesn't need to spell out certain boundaries. For example, he thinks it goes without saying that his mother shouldn't use name-calling when trying to make a point, or that it's inappropriate for her to listen to his voice mail without his consent. If she does these things, the situation immediately escalates to a point where Jonathon forgets that he is enforcing boundaries, and simply wants to *fight back.*

Or perhaps he knows these are things she might do, but he considers them "not important enough to argue over." Instead, he wants to set the "most important" boundaries first, that is, he wants her to cease the most drastic and hurtful behaviors.

Unfortunately, in either case, a more serious confrontation is likely to result if Jonathon overlooks these seemingly less significant acts.

There are two things Jonathon needs to keep in mind. First, *no* boundary "goes without saying" to someone with borderline personality disorder. Second, his boundaries will be far more effective if he works *up* to larger concepts.

The reason that setting small boundaries first is so much more effective is simple. If these smaller, simpler boundaries are respected, there will be *fewer* incidences of conflict. Conflicts often begin when simple boundaries are ignored, and behaviors escalate until everyone involved feels out of control. At that point, it becomes very difficult to enforce the previously defined boundary, the one that was considered so much "more important" than the simple courtesy.

Trying to enforce a boundary *during* an out of control situation usually isn't going to work. There's one exception, and it's an important one: maintaining your right to remove yourself *from* a situation that is out of control.

The next time Jonathon feels that a situation gets completely out of hand he should take the opportunity to look back at the actions and emotions that preceded the incident. More than likely Jonathon will recognize other boundaries that were crossed well before he felt a loss of control. Recognizing this, he may also realize that had those apparently insignificant boundaries been enforced, the conflict may have been defused or mitigated.

It's also wise to remember that you may not be able to enforce your boundaries in the most ideal way. If you say, "No more name calling," you must be prepared to end a conversation and disengage if name calling begins. It's frustrating—and it may be tempting to try and "make her stop" but you can't *make* her, and you can't *force* her. However, you don't have to *let* her call you names, either. Being able to walk away is a huge step in your own recovery from the trauma of being raised by a BPD mother.

Afterword

Success in Relationships with a BP

Improvement in the relationship with your mother will be hard won, and all the more fulfilling because of that. Every inch of ground you gain, as an individual and together, in the relationship, is something to be proud of.

Don't, however, fall into the temptation of measuring *your* success by *her* behavior. Of course, you will be encouraged by improvements in the way that she interacts with you, by the opportunity to form a healthier bond with her. But there is more to your success than that.

Through setting boundaries and engaging in validation and explanation, you are learning and growing into a more stable adult yourself. You're taking it upon yourself to learn the skills and self regulation *she* should have been teaching you, and instead was undermining. Your personal success doesn't depend upon whether or not she responds to these methods. Your success is measured by your *own* response to the situations you encounter. By becoming an individual capable of making the decisions you need to, for the reasons they need to be made, to continue your progress.

Having a borderline personality mother meant that your understanding of personal choice and self control were difficult to come by. Overcoming the abusive and traumatic effects she has and does have on your life can be a lifelong process. It is this process and your commitment to it by which you must measure your success, in which you must take pride.

It isn't your responsibility to cure her, nor *can* you cure her. Recovery contains an element of choice, when coping with borderline personality disorder. It's true that many borderlines want to get better and can respond very well to proper methods, but if she does not truly want to improve, or cannot without professional intervention, no amount of dedication or resolve on your part can force her to.

It's a bittersweet realization. She has spent much of her life trying to force people to do what she wants, and in the process you have learned that no one can force another person to behave or feel a certain way.

You can, however, dictate the boundaries of your own life and practice your own positive types of self-regulation. That is something to take pride in. It will serve you well in every relationship you have, even the one you have with yourself.

Hope's Story

I jumped when I heard the phone ring. It was a little after 11 PM, and I usually have an alarm set for 5:30 AM. Have to beat rush hour, after all. Friends don't call me this late.

I didn't get the jitters before I answered just because it was a late night call. I know for some people, the phone ringing so late makes them afraid of bad news. A car accident, a death, a sick kid in the emergency room, some twist of fate that makes calling at an unusual time a necessity.

But in my experience, it wasn't the news I had to be wary of, it was the caller.

Did I even want to get up and check the caller ID? Of course, because it *could* be an actual emergency of some kind, I had to.

My heart sank when I saw the number. It was a familiar one to me; at one time, it'd been *my* number, after all. It was my mom.

Again I debated with myself, in the space of two rings. Again, I sided with caution. I'd never forgive myself if something really had, for once, happened. I picked up.

To my surprise and cautious optimism, she wasn't drunk. There was no edge of meanness, or slyness. She asked how I was, and I answered and asked her, we chatted for a few minutes while I tried to gauge what was happening, what the catch was.

When she started in on a story about my nephew's first day of school, I interrupted. Something I wouldn't have done a couple months ago.

"Um, Mom? Do you..." I hesitated. Could I? Yes.

"Do you realize how late it is? I've really got to get a little sleep, but I'd love to talk to you again tomorrow?"

There was a pause. I flinched, and then scolded myself for it. I wasn't being disrespectful. I was just letting her know, politely, that I needed to get some rest.

"Oh my gosh, Hope. I'm so sorry! You know, it's the silliest thing, but with us talking practically every day, I've just... it just doesn't seem like you're so far away. I completely forgot about the time difference, Hope. Get to bed, missy! We'll talk tomorrow. Love you!"

I stammered a reply, assuring her it was fine, that I loved her too, and that we'd certainly talk tomorrow.

After I hung up I stared at the phone for a minute.

It seemed real. The memories that had triggered my rush of adrenaline, the fear I felt at the first ring of the phone came pouring in, and the contrast between those awful nights and this one...

I ran the tap for a glass of water, and carried it back to my bedroom, sat on my bed and drank it down in the dark. I'd spent many nights holding the phone, sweaty palmed, white knuckled, listening to my mother rant at me. Sometimes about me, sometimes about my sister.

I'd sat up for hours talking her down from suicide threats that I didn't think were real but couldn't dare take a chance on. I'd gone to work half-dead myself, many mornings, after an all night phone marathon listening to her drunkenly cry.

She just forgot about the time difference.

It had been months since she'd called me so late. Maybe a year since I'd first started standing up to her. I'd noticed, I'd hesitantly *allowed* myself to notice, that things were getting better, I thought. But when the phone rang with me tucked into bed, my first thought was that I'd been fooling myself or that I'd been in denial.

That I wasn't really strong enough to stand up for myself to begin with, that it couldn't possibly work.

I curled up under the blanket again, my spot still warm, and smiled. It was working. Oh, sure, there'd be more tough times. I knew that. But I'd told her I had to get off the phone, that I needed to sleep... I was strong enough. And she... had understood. Believed me, accepted that. She was trying. We both were.